TELEPHONE TECHNIQUES

Maria Pemberton

THE INDUSTRIAL SOCIETY

*First published August 1986 by
The Industrial Society
Robert Hyde House,
48 Bryanston Square,
London W1H 7LN
Telephone: 071-262 2401*

Reprinted 1988, 1990, 1991

© *The Industrial Society 1986*

ISBN 0 85290 383 9

**Printed by Reedprint Limited,
Windsor, Berkshire, England**

All rights reserved. No part of this publication may be reproduced, stored in a retrieval system or transmitted, in any form or by any means, electronic, mechanical, photocopying, recording and/or otherwise without the prior written permission of the publishers. This book may not be lent, resold, hired out or otherwise disposed of by way of trade in any form, binding or cover other than that in which it is published, without prior consent of the publishers.

CONTENTS

Foreword

1	**Introduction**	1
2	**Communicating over the telephone**	3
	Listening	3
	Voice	4
3	**Developing good telephone skills**	6
	Preparation	6
	Control	7
	Transferring calls	9
	Follow-up action after the call	10
	Making calls	10
4	**Difficult calls and difficult callers**	11
5	**Taking messages**	14
6	**The role of the telephonist**	16
7	**Conclusion**	18
	Appendix 1 **Message pad**	19
	Appendix 2 **Industrial Society services**	20

FOREWORD

Over 70 per cent of the initial contacts in business begin on the telephone. Skilful use of the telephone often determines the degree of success or failure of both the organisation and the individual.

This book is based on the considerable experience of The Industrial Society in being involved with people at work in companies, in running telephone skills courses, and helping those who use the telephone for business. It contains guidelines, checklists and practical examples for action. These will prove invaluable aids to all people who use the telephone, such as managers at all levels, secretaries and all those involved in sales. The voice on the telephone reflects the image of the organisation and should be positive and professional.

YVONNE BENNION
Division Director

1 INTRODUCTION

Most of us have to use the telephone at work either to respond to people's enquiries or to obtain information from others.

Very often the telephone is the only point of contact we have with our customers. How each of us treats callers will therefore affect the way in which our organisation is seen. The process does not stop with the telephonist — it continues with all of us whenever we answer our telephone.

Most of us would agree that we want to create an image of ourselves and of our organisation which is helpful, efficient and friendly. Unfortunately this does not always happen for a variety of reasons. Some of these are given below:

- not returning calls when you said you would
- not answering promptly
- eating, drinking, smoking on the telephone — it can all be heard
- leaving people hanging on without keeping them informed of what is happening
- not being prepared to tell the caller your name
- holding two conversations at once
- asking the caller to call back
- transferring people round and round the organisation
- unintelligible greetings or just saying 'hello' when answering
- negative attitude
- sounding unsure of what you are saying.

It is also far easier to be evasive, petulant and even rude on the telephone than it is when we are face to face with someone.

Because of the busy working lives most of us lead, it is also easy to see the telephone as an interruption. How frustrating it is when it rings when we are half way through adding a column of figures or writing a difficult letter. That irritation can be heard in our voice.

However much we feel this piece of machinery is a distraction, it is vital for continuing the prosperity of our organisation. Seventy per cent of new business is initiated

1

over the telephone. Can any of us therefore afford to leave things to chance?

Creating the right image on the telephone is helped by a number of factors:

- establishing a good telephone procedure in the organisation
- establishing consistency in the way the telephone is answered throughout the organisation
- including 'how to use the telephone' in induction sessions for all new employees.

There is no doubt that if everyone in the organisation adopts the right approach to the telephone, we will be seen as the efficient, friendly and helpful organisation we want to be.

2 COMMUNICATING OVER THE TELEPHONE

A simple definition of communication is

> 'The creation of understanding in someone else's mind, in order to promote action.'

Communication is a two-way process and the understanding we aim to create must be accurate in every way.

When we talk to people face to face we have the great advantage of being able to see them. This helps because we can actually see how they are responding to our message. We can easily recognise the 'glazed look' when someone has not quite grasped our meaning and we can act on that and try saying it in a different way until we are satisfied we have got the message across.

On the telephone we are hampered because all the visual contact has gone (at least until a telephone with a video screen is invented). We therefore have to rely on two crucial elements:

- listening and concentrating on what we hear
- our voice — its tone and the words we use.

Listening

When we are on the telephone to someone, we are either speaking or listening. We often regard speaking as an active process and listening as a passive one. However, **listening well** can be a lot more difficult than speaking, and requires a lot more effort.

On the telephone it is just as easy to stop listening, for various reasons:

- having pre-conceived ideas about what the caller is going to say
- something distracting us in the office
- the caller having an uninteresting voice
- panicking because of our own inexperience.

One of the best solutions to poor listening is to concentrate our minds on the subject matter by taking notes.

Have a telephone pad and pen next to the telephone at all times and if necessary fix them in some way to the desk so they do not get lost. There is nothing more frustrating than scrabbling around for something to write on or with after the call has started. Taking notes right from the beginning of the conversation saves repeating small but vital facts later on and minimises the effect of distractions going on around us.

Finally we need to make sure the caller knows that we are listening. When speaking face to face we use many non-verbal signs to indicate this, such as nodding. On the telephone we need to use **'verbal nods'**. For example, we need to say **'I see'**, **'yes'**, **'okay'**, **'right'** or **'mmm'** to indicate:

- that we are still there, and
- that we are listening.

Voice

As we have no visual contact on the telephone we cannot use non-verbal body signs to help attract and keep the listener's attention; we have only *our voice*. However, it is not just what we say (words) but the way we say it (tone) that is important in creating the right image. We need to capitalise on these two elements to make up for the loss of visual contact.

Words are the tools of a speaker's trade and we should bear the following points in mind if we are to be successful. Use words which

- form pictures in the mind of the listener. For example, instead of saying 'hold on' and disappearing, try 'I need to check that in our files, but it shouldn't take a moment.'
- are jargon free and pitched at the level of the caller. A typical example follows:

   Caller: "Can I speak to your Accounts Department?"

   Us: "Is it bought ledger or sales ledger you want?"

   Since most people do not know the difference we should reply

   "Yes, what is it in connection with?"

- are not colloquial or too familiar. Avoid things like 'Guv' or 'lovie'. Show respect to the caller.
- are positive and helpful. Avoid negative words like 'busy', 'try' and 'don't know'. Instead try 'I will find someone who can help you,' or 'Can I call you back in ten minutes when I have found the answer?'

Tone of voice conveys the way we are feeling about the conversation, the caller or the way we feel on that particular day. The following positive and negative emotions can all be conveyed by our voice:

- enthusiastic or bored
- tired or alert
- aggressive or calm
- confident or unsure.

One good way of making sure we sound right is to smile when we are talking. Smiling relaxes the vocal chords and has a dramatic effect on the voice, instantly making us sound more friendly and relaxed.

It is, however, crucial that when the phone rings we try and put everything out of our mind and concentrate on the person on the other end of the phone. In this way we can avoid sounding harassed, annoyed, or conveying any number of negative emotions.

We need to adopt the right approach to using the telephone before we start. We need to listen carefully and adopt a positive and professional approach in our choice of words and the way we sound. **And don't forget to smile!**

3 DEVELOPING TELEPHONE SKILLS

When we answer the telephone, we are the organisation, and developing good skills will help make sure that people will want to deal with our organisation and us personally in the future.

The only difference between a business call and calling a friend for a chat is that with the business call there is usually a specific purpose to be achieved.

To achieve the purpose of the call there are three main areas which need consideration:
- preparing for the call
- controlling the call
- following up action agreed after the call has finished.

Preparing for calls

We may think we can prepare nothing in advance before picking up the telephone when it rings. However, to provide an efficient service there is a lot of background work needed.

For receiving calls we need all the following:

- A good knowledge of our organisation, its products or services and our colleagues. It is difficult when we first start in a job to know all this but to some extent we must find out ourselves. We should try to

    read brochures on our organisation
    meet and get to know as many people as possible and what they do in the organisation
    find out thoroughly what happens in our own department or section.

- An up-to-date internal telephone directory. This again can be usefully cross-referenced to particular functions and alternative people if one number is engaged.
- A pad and pen fixed near the phone. A simple message pad can be useful. The rules for message-taking are given in Chapter 5.

- Our organisation's brochures if we are involved in informing customers about our products and services.

A good way to add to our background knowledge is simply to ask our colleagues lots of questions. If we do not know the answer to a caller's request, we should not simply transfer the call to someone else. We should also find out the answer ourselves later, so we will be able to help next time.

Controlling calls

There are a number of golden rules which apply to all incoming calls, whether from within the organisation or from outside.

Answer promptly

There is nothing worse when ringing someone than to hear the phone ring for ages. A good standard is three or four rings. This rule applies to other people's telephones when they are not there. It is not enough to assume you will not be able to help — think of the person at the other end — they would rather hear a voice than end up putting the phone down in frustration.

Give a greeting

This should consist of:

>'Good morning/afternoon
>Our Department
>Our name'

eg: 'Good morning, Accounts Department, Felicity Brown speaking.'

From this greeting, the caller can identify whether they are through to the right department and also have a friendly voice quite happy to say who they are. Interestingly enough, when we answer like this, callers respond immediately by telling us their name. This is useful to acquire early on because we can then use that person's name throughout the call, ie

'I'll make sure you receive the information by tomorrow, **Mr Jones**'.

This again sounds tremendously friendly and helpful.

Use appropriate questions to maintain control

There are basically two types of questions — open and closed. Open questions are those which require more than a straight 'yes' or 'no'. They begin with — who, where, when, how, why, what. Closed questions, conversely, require a 'yes/no' answer. They generally start — did you, was it, have you, etc. We need to use the appropriate questioning techniques to elicit the relevant information from the caller, ie

'Did you want more information on that?' may just get 'yes'.

'What more information would you like on that?' You will get specifics.

Keep people informed

If for any reason we have to leave our caller holding on, it is crucial that we keep them informed of what is happening. We should tell them how long we will be and if appropriate offer to call them back with the information they require.

Never .... hold two conversations ....

It doesn't matter what else is happening in the office, even if our boss is breathing down our neck, the person on the other end of the phone deserves our sole attention, so try to ignore everything else but the caller.

Check all details

Names, phone numbers, addresses, and any other details should always be repeated back to the caller to make sure we have got it right.

Summarise action

A useful way of closing the call is to summarise to the caller what is going to happen next, eg

'I will make sure our Accounts Department contacts you by Monday.'

'I will send you our catalogue in the post tonight.'

'If you could post the details to me tonight, first class post, I will make sure you have our proposal by Friday.'

It is important in the summary to set deadlines for when any action must happen. Of course, having done that we must make sure we stick to that deadline. Nothing sounds more haphazard than

'I'll let you have the information sometime next week.'

So this is another way in which we can sound organised and impressive.

These are the **seven golden rules** which apply to all telephone calls. However, we are often involved in transferring calls to someone else in the organisation and this again needs to be handled efficiently.

Transferring calls

If you have ever been transferred round and round an organisation, having to repeat your story, you will know what a frustrating experience this is. By following the guidelines below we can ensure our callers are dealt with efficiently.

- Know your telephone system thoroughly. With the varied or different telephone systems available we need to know which buttons to press to transfer calls.
- Tell the caller what is happening. Tell them the name and extension number of the person you are transferring them to, so that if they do get cut off they can get back to the right person.
- When you have got the person you wish to transfer the call to on the line, give them the relevant information. Don't just put the call through saying nothing. Tell them the caller's name, company and request briefly.
- If you receive a transferred call you can, armed with the information above, greet the caller thus:

  'Good afternoon, Mr Taylor, Susan Brown here. I understand you need some information on word processing software.'

  This sounds much better than simply, 'Hello can I help you?'
- If the person we wish to transfer the call to is engaged

or unavailable we should give the caller options on how to proceed:

> to hold until the person is free
> to leave a message with you for the right person to ring back.

- If the caller opts to hold, keep going back to them to tell them what is happening. Do give them a chance to reply. If the wait becomes lengthy, they may decide to ring back later.

Follow-up action after the call

The most important point here is that we ensure the things we promised do happen.

If we said someone else will ring the caller back we must make sure that they do. Unfortunately if this does not happen, it leaves the caller with the impression of inefficiency.

Making calls

We can often prepare much more thoroughly before we make a telephone call ourselves, and here it is just as important to remember our aim of being helpful, friendly and efficient.

There are various stages:

- Identify the purpose of the call clearly. We must clear our minds thoroughly before we start.
- If we have various things we wish to cover it is wise to make some notes to make sure nothing has been missed. If necessary we should devise a simple record pad.
- Consider the time of day we are making the call. There are two reasons for this. Calls in the UK are cheaper after 1.00 pm. It is a good idea therefore, to plan to make all but urgent outgoing calls in the afternoon.

    Secondly, we need to consider the person we are calling. A lengthy call at 4.45 pm on a Friday afternoon may not be well received. Certainly if we are making calls abroad we need to make sure the person we want will actually be at work because of the time differences.

4 DIFFICULT CALLS AND DIFFICULT CALLERS

Many things can go wrong during a telephone call — some are due to difficult people and some are quite simply caused by mechanical problems. Both types of difficulty need to be approached professionally. The points below may help to overcome some of the most common problems.

Many telephone systems have lots of special functions enabling us to store telephone numbers in a memory, programme the telephone to keep dialling a number until we get through, and so on. Many of these functions can help us so we need to familiarise ourselves with the scope (or limitations) of our system.

There are mechanical difficulties, however, with all telephones that are somewhat out of our control, for example:

- crossed lines
- being cut off
- bad lines where we cannot hear the other person clearly
- wrong numbers.

Let us look at these in more detail and consider the best way of dealing with them if they arise.

Crossed lines

We can usually tell when someone dials in on our call. Often the dialling makes it impossible for us to continue speaking. When the interference stops, we should establish whether anyone else is on the line by saying: 'I think we have a crossed line' and by suggesting, politely, that they should redial.

Being cut off

It is generally accepted that if we get cut off, the person who initiated the call should redial. However, if it is an important client and we have their telephone number, it is a good idea to ring them back. However, when we start the conversation again, we should avoid getting bogged down discussing whose fault it was that we got cut off.

Bad lines

If a line really is bad, it is better to explain as clearly as possible that we will call back.

Wrong numbers

Even if we have dialled the right number, we can sometimes find ourselves through to the wrong one. If in doubt, we should ask the other person if they are the 'XYZ Company' and give them the number we dialled. We should not expect them to tell us their number. Since there are many odd calls which people get, particularly at home, many of us are reluctant to tell apparent strangers our telephone number.

Difficult callers

Apart from these obvious mechanical problems, we can face a lot of other difficulties with the callers themselves.

Probably the caller we all most dread is the rude, aggressive person who more often than not is complaining about something. Apart from the need to remain professional in the face of extreme adversity, the following tips are also crucial:

Do

- Accept responsibility for whatever is being complained about. You are the organisation to the caller, and there is nothing worse than saying things like 'It's always happening, this sort of thing' or 'Yes, they're hopeless in that section' or worse still 'You're the tenth person this week who's complained about that'.
- Apologise

- Avoid taking any insults personally. Often people complaining just want to get it off their chest and once they have calmed down we can deal with the problem constructively.
- Finish the call positively by telling the caller what will happen next.
- Take follow-up action immediately and make sure you ring back if you said you would.

Efficient handling of complaints can often result in a pleased and impressed customer who will come back to us again.

Three other techniques can also be useful in dealing with difficult callers.

Questions

Using the right combination of open and closed questions can determine the type of response we get. For example if we have a caller who does not seem to be able to get to the point, asking open questions could make the situation worse. If we ask a series of closed questions we may get to the purpose of the call more quickly.

Alternatives

Offering alternatives to the caller can sometimes help us as well as them. If, for example, we cannot get the information a caller wants, saying 'would you like to hold on, or shall I call you back' can help. Callers can then decide for themselves, rather than us deciding for them.

Using the caller's name

As we have said already, giving our name when we answer the phone immediately prompts callers to give us theirs.

Using the caller's name is a good way of interrupting. If we have a rather vague, waffly caller, by the interjection of — 'Mrs Lewis, did you send the goods back?' we can get the caller's attention and follow-up with a closed question to keep control of the call.

Finally, the most important thing to do when dealing with difficult callers is to treat them as we would like to be treated if we were them, ie politely and efficiently.

5 TAKING MESSAGES

We have devoted an entire chapter to this activity. One of the major complaints from people at work in this whole area is that people simply do not ring back.

Unfortunately, if we take a message for someone and they do not ring back it is our fault, and that is how the caller will see it. They will probably assume the message was not passed on and they will therefore blame us.

So, how can we ensure that messages are dealt with promptly and efficiently?

There are three stages to effective message taking, all equally important.

- Being prepared.
- Taking the message.
- Making sure it is dealt with.

Being prepared

At the outset, it must be said that offering to take a message is the lowest form of help. We should only offer to do this when we have explored all the other avenues. Many people, when answering someone else's phone simply say: 'I'm sorry he's out, can I take a message?. That is not helpful. Instead we should say:

'I'm sorry, he is out. Can I help at all?' and very often we can, and the call is dealt with there and then.

However, for those occasions when we do have to take a message, we should be armed with a suitable message pad.

It is important to use a special pad or form, otherwise important messages get lost among the papers on someone's desk. It is preferable to have them printed on coloured paper, so they stand out.

Many people design their own pads and have them duplicated, so they can make sure the right information is received. See Appendix 1 for an example.

Taking the message

We have already said that if we take down any information like telephone numbers, names and so on, we should repeat them to the caller to make sure they are correct.

We should also note down what action we have said will be taken. If we have said someone will call back this afternoon, we must make sure that the person dealing with the message both knows and does that.

Finally, make sure the person you are passing the message onto can read your writing.

Making sure the message is actioned

Having taken the message, the next step is to make sure something happens about it. It is important, therefore, to leave it in a prominent place where it will be seen. Many organisations have message boards in each department or section so that all messages can be pinned up. Certainly, try to avoid just adding your message to someone's in-tray. It may get covered by incoming post.

If you are going to be out of the office for any length of time, tell either the switchboard or a colleague who sits nearby how long you will be. This will help them to deal with your calls efficiently. Above all if you receive a message — do carry out the action promised.

6 THE ROLE OF THE TELEPHONIST

The telephonist's role in creating the initial impression of the organisation is absolutely crucial. The importance of the telephonist cannot be overstressed. We have already looked at the way other staff should answer calls — the same rules apply to the telephonist.

Say 'good morning/afternoon' first, followed by the name of the organisation and perhaps 'may I help you?' The smile in the voice is vital here. Because the telephonist is so important to the organisation it is also wise to help that person do their job well. Every organisation can do this by laying down the ground rules that must be adhered to.

For example:

- Give priority to incoming calls.
- Give a clear greeting (as above).
- Tell the caller that they are being put through
    - eg 'Putting you through' or
    - 'It's ringing for you'.
- Reassure waiting callers they are not forgotten.
- If the extension is engaged or not being answered ask if you can put them through to another in the same department or someone who can take a message.
- Be helpful and friendly — the caller is relying on you.
- Listen carefully and be responsive.
- Don't tell callers through the tone of your voice, or in actual words — how many calls there are so you can't spend time with them. If you control the call with effective questions, that will cut down the time wasted considerably.

Practical aids for the telephonist

It is most important that the telephonist should have up-to-date information about the organisation. Make sure you know or have for quick and easy reference the following information:

- Names and locations of the chairman, managing direc-

tor, executives, managers, their deputies and secretaries.
- All departments and their functions — so help can be offered immediately to a vague enquirer and they can be put through to the right person.

Gaining cooperation from extension users

The relationship between telephonists and extension users is not always as it should be. In some organisations it is almost tradition to complain about telephonists — easy targets who are often situated in an isolated place, unknown by name to many staff and unable to answer their accusers.

Ideally, telephonists should be able to explain in person to extension users how they can help to provide an efficient service. This would be useful to include in the induction programme of new employees. If this is not possible, and even if it is, instructions from the telephonist can be listed alongside instructions on how to use your extension. Some points you might include are:

- Telephonist's priority is to answer incoming calls, please be patient if you need the telephonist for any reason during the particularly busy period of 10.00-11.30 and 14.00-15.30.
- Please inform the telephonist if there is not going to be anybody in your office during a certain period and where calls should be directed, or programme your phone to automatically transfer to someone who will take messages if you are leaving the office. But remember to tell whomever it is that you are doing this.
- Please look up your own numbers wherever possible.
- Let the telephonist know if someone has:
    changed their job/responsibilities within the organisation
    left
    changed their extension number
    or is about to join.
- Please inform the telephonist of temporary staff working in the building and of their extension number.

If the telephonists do not have all the information they need, it is important to go and find out.

7 CONCLUSION

If you were to telephone ten organisations now, how many would impress you with good telephone practice?

For example:
- How long until the operator answered?
- How were you answered?
- How long until you were connected?
- Were you connected to the right person/department?
- Were you passed from pillar to post?
- Was it a pleasure to deal with the company by telephone or was it frustrating?

Can your organisation pass the 'telephone test'?

The telephone plays a vital part in any business. Properly arranged and efficiently operated it is a major asset. Misused, it wastes time and money, but even more important, it can lose business. There is a definite skill in using the telephone effectively, particularly in business.

REMEMBER — efficient telephone practice reflects an efficient business organisation.

APPENDIX 1
MESSAGE PAD

Message for: ....

Taken by: ....

Date and time: ....

Message:

Please call back by: ....

They will call back: ....

APPENDIX 2
INDUSTRIAL SOCIETY SERVICES

The Industrial Society runs a number of courses on the skills of communicating, including speaking and listening on the telephone.

Titles include:

Receptionists and telephonists
Customer relations — using the telephone
Experienced secretary
Senior secretary in management today
Developing the secretary's role
Telephone selling — an introduction
Telephone selling — cold calling

The Communications Skills Department runs public and in-house courses on:

Interviewing — the practical skills
Interviewing — the selection techniques
Meetings — chairing and participating
Minutes and agendas
Report writing
Letter writing
Speaking to groups
Speaking in management
Communication skills at work
Rapid and effective reading

Further information on any of these courses is available from the Communications Skills Department, Peter Runge House, 3 Carlton House Terrace, London SW1Y 5DG. Telephone: 071-839 4300.